CW00645736

ESSEX THAMES-SIDE

WOOLWICH TO THORPE BAY

ESSEX THAMES-SIDE

WOOLWICH TO THORPE BAY

CHRIS THURMAN

TEMPUS

Two Thames barges photographed from Canvey Island in 1975. These barges were part of a cavalcade of tall ships and other vessels moving from London Docks to the Thames Estuary and the sea. More details about the age and design of Thames barges are given in chapter 5.

Frontispiece: Fishing boats at sunset, Leigh-on-Sea, 1964. Leigh is a traditional fishing village near the mouth of the Thames, its fleet specialising in shellfish. More details about this fishing industry are given in chapters 7 and 8. This photograph was taken just after sunset, and encapsulates for me the wonderful mood of the river at this time of the day at this super location.

First published 2004

© Chris Thurman, 2004

The right of Chris Thurman to be identified as the Author of this work has been asserted in accordance with the Copyrights, Designs and Patents Act 1988.

All rights reserved. No part of this book may be reprinted or reproduced or utilised in any form or by any electronic, mechanical or other means, now known or hereafter invented, including photocopying and recording, or in any information storage or retrieval system, without the permission in writing from the Publishers.

British Library Cataloguing in Publication Data.
A catalogue record for this book is available from the British Library.

ISBN 0 7524 3232 X

Typesetting and origination by Tempus Publishing.
Printed in Great Britain.

CONTENTS

ACKNOWLEDGEMENTS AND REFERENCES

Firstly, I would like to thank my wife Gill, for her support and for keeping me company on many trips around this area when I was checking on where the old photographs had been taken and what changes had occurred since. My thanks are also due to Campbell McCutcheon of Tempus for his encouragement in producing this book, I also want to congratulate Emma Jackson of Tempus for the splendid design of this book. My third Tempus thank you is to Wendy Tse. My thanks also go to Peter Owen for his many thoughts and for the history of the Palace Hotel, and to Tom Moss and the many ex-students who helped me with the short history of Dagenham County High. Finally, I want to thank Tony Meddle MBE for all his help regarding the Leigh chapters. Tony has spent his entire working life in the Leigh fishing industry, being awarded the Silver Medal in 1977 by the White Fish Authority and then receiving an MBE in 1995 for services to the shellfish industry. Without Tony's help the Leigh chapters would have been very thin; sadly, Tony did not live to see this book published.

I used many different references during the preparation of this book, and there are some really splendid local histories. However, these books are specific to particular places whereas *Essex Thames-side* has a much wider geographical coverage. One of the most entertaining, although very dated, is Arthur Mee's *Essex*, which was published by Hodder and Stoughton in 1940 as part of the *King's England* series, although my edition was printed in 1951.

INTRODUCTION

My first book, *London's River*, covered the stretch of the river Thames from Woolwich to Westminster and contained photographs taken by me from the mid-1950s to 2002. This book continues the coverage downriver, from Woolwich to Southend-on-Sea, which is the northern or Essex side of the river.

I lived in Barking for several decades and went to school in Dagenham. Southend-on-Sea and Leigh-on-Sea were only a short drive away and we visited them in all seasons when the weather was fine. It was thus inevitable that as a young, eager photographer I took shots in all these communities as well as some of the areas in between.

ESSEX THAMES-SIDE DEFINED

There was a major change in the structure of local government in April 1965 when the Greater London Council (GLC) was established. At that time Barking and Dagenham, which had both been Essex boroughs, were united to form the London Borough of Barking and photographs of the last and first mayors of each regime appear in chapter 2. East Ham (which contains North Woolwich) was a county borough until 1965 when it also became subsumed in the GLC. Nevertheless, in purely county terms East Ham was generally considered to be part of Essex.

The book therefore covers part of what is now the Greater London area, as well as Essex itself. More specifically it refers to the following boroughs:

GREATER LONDON AREA

NAME	1999 POPULATION	COMMENTS
Newham	236,000	The only area of Newham photographed in this book is the part around Woolwich and Beckton.
Barking and Dagenham	156,000	Photographs include rail and other links with Southend-on-Sea.
Havering	231,000	Although bordering the Thames, there are no photographs from this borough in the book.

COUNTY OF ESSEX

NAME	1999 POPULATION	COMMENTS
Thurrock*	135,000	Includes Grays, Tilbury and Purfleet.
Castle Point	85,000	Includes Canvey Island.
Southend-on-Sea*	177,000	Includes Leigh-on-Sea, Chalkwell, Westcliff-on-Sea and Thorpe Bay.

* A unitary authority. Southend-on-Sea used to be a county borough, but following yet another reorganisation of local government in 1973 it lost this status. More recently, it has become a unitary authority.

Two other boroughs lying close to this area in Essex are Basildon (population 166,000) and Rochford (population 78,000). Although neither borough abuts the Thames, they could nevertheless be said to be part of the Thames-side conurbation.

TWO GROWING CENTRES OF POPULATION

London gradually spread eastwards and merged with boroughs located in Essex. This was undoubtedly due to the construction of the Royal Docks, but it also reflected population growth. At one time East Ham and Barking were quite separate entities, but early in the twentieth century they became a part of the Greater London area. House building continued and finally the Greater London area extended well into Essex to include such boroughs as Dagenham, Ilford and Romford. The opening of the Ford Motor Works led to a great house-building programme in Dagenham.

In comparison to London, Southend-on-Sea developed late as a town. Indeed, a few hundred years ago it was a small hamlet called South End; the main population centre was Prittlewell, and South End was so-called because it was at the southern end of Prittlewell. However, around the end of the eighteenth century Southend started to develop and among the first buildings were the Royal Hotel and a group of houses in what is now called Royal Terrace. It was the coming of the railway that made a substantial difference to Southend's fortunes. Up to the time of the railway it had taken one and a half days to sail from central London to Southend. With the coming of the railway this journey time was cut to one and a half hours! The railway company exploited this quantum leap in time reduction by keeping fares low, and so a new concept developed – the day tripper.

By the end of the nineteenth century, Southend had started to move westwards. There was eventually an eastward expansion to Thorpe Bay, but the westward movement was to develop first Westcliff and then Chalkwell. This major expansion eventually reached the small fishing community of Leigh. Leigh had a very long maritime history, indeed the *Mayflower* had called there, but it was eventually merged with Southend. Prittlewell, for so long the main centre in the area, was subsumed within the Southend area.

So, at both ends of Essex Thames-side there were two growing population centres, one moving westwards and the other eastwards. Added to this was the movement of many thousands of people, particularly after 1945, from East London and the old Essex boroughs such as Barking and Ilford to places such as Brentwood, Billericay, Rayleigh and Chelmsford. Between these two centres there was, inevitably, some ribbon development along the two main roads, the A13 and A127.

This led to many economic and social links between the two population centres, one of which is shown in another photograph,

namely the 'Kursaal Flyer'. This was a carnival float specially designed by Southend Council to participate in carnivals in towns in the proximity of Southend. It was a publicity measure.

INDUSTRY

Virtually the whole of the river from Woolwich to Canvey Island is flanked by industrial activities of various kinds. The river was a major trunk route for the carriage of large bulky raw materials or for the transport of finished manufactured products. Thus electric power stations, a gas production centre, oil refining and storage facilities and Ford Motor Company were all located on the river. In no way can this stretch of Essex Thames-side be said to be pretty. Public access to the river is simply not possible for long stretches of the riverbank due to this industrial activity and that in turn impinges upon the range of photographs in this book.

LEIGH FISHING INDUSTRY AND LEISURE

At Canvey the river frontage changes. Part of Canvey is industrialised and then it becomes an area of riverside walks, marinas and sailing clubs. After this comes the traditional fishing village of Leigh-on-Sea. Leigh has a nautical history going back many centuries, and its shellfish fishing industry is quite unique for this part of Essex.

The river frontage changes yet again after Leigh, with the leisure use of the river having high priority. Indeed, the leisure activities commence in Leigh and there are many yacht clubs between this village and Thorpe Bay, which is several miles further downriver towards its mouth. Southend-on-Sea has a wide range of leisure facilities, as can be seen from the photographs.

TRANSPORT LINKS

Mention has already been made of day trips to Southend. For many years these were rail based, and while the book gives prominence to the Fenchurch Street to Southend line, there has also been a second routing via Stratford, Ilford, Romford, Brentwood and Shenfield to Southend Victoria. The two routes have always been run by different companies, going back to the pre-nationalisation days; the Fenchurch Street line was run by LMS (London, Midland and Scottish) and the Southend Victoria line was run by LNER (London North Eastern Railway).

However, the development of the motor vehicle gave an extra travel dimension, and more and more day trippers visited Southend by car or by coach. There are two main roads to Southend – the A13 (which is given prominence in this book) and the A127 Southend arterial road. The latter road was one of the first roads specifically designed to meet the needs of the growing road traffic; it was one of the first roads to have a double carriageway and was opened in the 1920s.

DAY TRIPPERS

Where did the day trippers come from? Primarily from East London and the Essex boroughs which are now part of the Greater London Authority. My family was one of those that went to Southend several times a year, at weekends when the weather looked good. Indeed, we went in the old Ford 8 model Y (see photograph), although climbing 'Bread and Cheese' hill could be interesting in this small car. My father had bought the car before 1939, but it could not be used during the war because petrol was not available to the general public. Petrol became available in 1945 (albeit still strictly rationed) and virtually our first post-war car journey was to Southend-on-Sea.

Day trips continue to this day. While I was gathering data for this book we went to Southend and parked near the Rossi restaurant in Westcliff (see photograph) and went in for a coffee. It was mid-morning on a sunny February weekday. I was surprised at how many people were employed by Rossi's on that day, but within half an hour of our arrival there was a queue of people waiting for coffee and teas. The 'grey market', defined by the colour of their hair, was there in force.

ECONOMIC AND SOCIAL CHANGE

The photographs in this book cover a period of over forty years and inevitably they reflect many economic and social changes. Among the changes highlighted by the photographs in this book are:

– Decline of traditional industries. Beckton Gasworks, Barking Power Station, Shell Haven oil refinery and the Blue Circle cement works – all have ceased operation. Even the Ford Motor Company has stopped making cars at Dagenham.

– Decline of ocean-going passenger transport.

– Growth of containerised cargo.

– Growth of shopping and the advent of shopping malls.

– Change in fashions, and within that a change to more casual dress.

– Growth of restaurants and eating away from home. There is one photograph taken in Westcliff that shows a whole row of Italian restaurants, as well as the restaurants 'under the arches' in both Westcliff and Southend.

– Eating out of doors. This is another remarkable change; it is as if, nowadays, the British want to be a café society and the only problem is the weather. Nevertheless, on a recent sunny weekday in February many restaurants on the front at Westcliff had tables out of doors, albeit surrounded by plastic windbreaks. Where did this drive to be a café society come from? The photographs in this book (with a couple of exceptions) start from 1959/60, which is also about the same time that package holidays to the sun started. Tour operators were able to combine the speed of modern jet aircraft with new hotels and guaranteed sunshine in places like Spain, Italy and Greece at prices highly competitive to hotels and boarding houses in this country. Quite suddenly millions of Britons started to travel to the sun, and have continued to do so in ever greater numbers.

– Decline of traditional UK seaside holidays. This is a second effect of package holidays, and hotels have either closed or been forced to seek customers in other guises, e.g. special rates for weekends, use for business conferences or convention centres. Of the three traditional-style hotels in Southend-on-Sea, only one remains operational as such (the Westcliff); the Royal is now a pub and the beautifully sited and designed Palace meets local social needs.

– Growth of road traffic. There are several photographs in this book that show a relatively open road. In fact the growth in usage of cars since 1960 has been quite dramatic as statistics show. In 1961 only 30 per cent of households had a car, but in 1998 the number had increased to 70 per cent. An alternative way of measuring road usage is to look at the total distance travelled. This concept is known as 'vehicle kilometres' and between 1960 and 1998 the figure increased 4.6 times. The road congestion seen today is therefore not surprising.

—   Growth of motorways – the most obvious example in this book is the Dartford crossing. The first Dartford Tunnel had one bore and opened in 1963, however traffic growth was such that eventually the Queen Elizabeth II Bridge was constructed and opened in 1991.

THE FUTURE AND FINAL THOUGHTS

The Thames Gateway plan is just one of the ideas put forward to help regenerate part of this area. There are two other proposals which are currently under consideration, both of which have critics. These are the London Gateway proposal to redevelop the Shell Haven site into a container port, and the proposal to develop London Southend airport. In addition, the entrance to Southend Pier is being rebuilt.

The photographs in this book cover a period exceeding four decades and they record a number of changes. Some have already been mentioned in this introduction, while others will become evident through the description of photographs later in the book. These changes have had a major impact on the look of the area, its transport infrastructure and its industrial activity. Furthermore, these changes have all occurred within living memory.

Inevitably, this book is not a complete record of Essex Thames-side. Nevertheless, I hope that it does show many facets of this stretch of the Thames and its northern bank.

Chris Thurman, MBE
February 2004

This photograph was taken in Longbridge Road, Barking, in the early 1960s. There is very little traffic and no yellow lines to control parking – a situation so different from 2004! The car on the right is a Hillman Minx, while the letters DER on the van show that it was used by a television rental company.

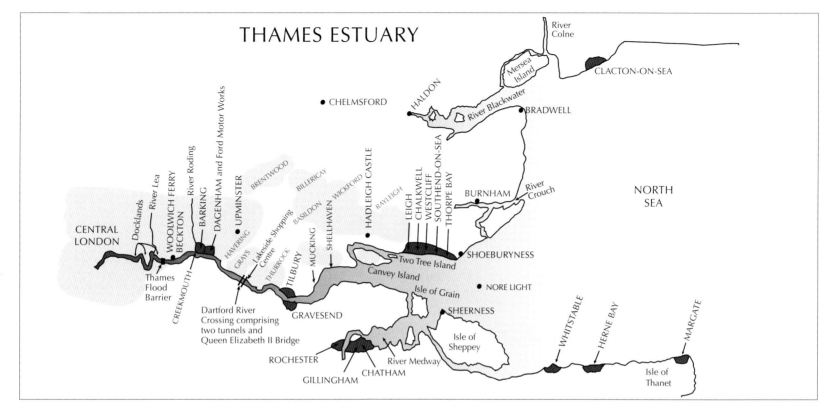

This map shows the river Thames from central London to its estuary, and the land lying on the northern bank is the topic of this book. More specifically, the places covered start at Woolwich and then move downstream until they reach Southend-on-Sea and Thorpe Bay.

Where the mouth of the river actually lies is a moot point. It is generally taken to be the Nore Light, but I recently attended a lecture on the Essex coastline during which it was suggested that its mouth could be a line between Clacton (in Essex) and Whitstable (in Kent). Another point made during the same lecture, by a leading Essex archaeologist, was that before the last Great Ice Age, some 15,000 years ago, the Thames had actually been a tributary of the Rhine.

Opposite: Tug *Sun III* operating in Royal Albert Dock, 1970. The Royal Docks comprised the Royal Victoria, the Royal Albert and the King George V Docks, and in 1970 they were fully operational as can be seen opposite. Prince Albert opened the Royal Victoria Dock in 1855, while the Royal Albert became operational in 1880, and the King George V Dock was finally opened in 1921.

The Royal Group of Docks was the last to be built in Central London and covered 245 acres. It is claimed that they formed the largest confined dock area in the world and could handle virtually all the large ocean-going ships built in the twentieth century. The Royals were the last of the upriver docks to close, in 1981. After some barren years, the area around the Royal Docks has been extensively redeveloped, as shown on the following pages.

Before the reform of London's local government in 1965, these docks lay within the County Borough of East Ham, which was then considered to be within the County of Essex. It is therefore logical to include this area within a book dealing with the Essex bank of the Thames, and is an appropriate starting point for this journey down the Thames to Southend-on-Sea and Thorpe Bay.

CHAPTER 1
WOOLWICH AND
LAND ROUTES

Above: Royal Albert Dock, 1970. This is how it had been for decades, but it was to change forever within ten years. After their closure, the only docks still operated by the Port of London Authority were downriver at Tilbury (see chapter 3).

Below: Royal Albert Dock, 1995. The viewpoint is almost precisely the same as the photograph above and where there were once ships there is space. Canary Wharf Tower is clearly visible, and the tall, more distant building to the right is the NatWest Tower. The area to the left of the dock has been converted into London City Airport – the terminal buildings are just visible. However, even this view is now out of date and not only because of subsequent building. This photograph was taken from the old road, but there is now a new road bridge that crosses the dock and effectively obscures this view. The photographs on the opposite page were taken from the new bridge.

Above: An aeroplane taking off in 2003 from London City Airport, which specialises in handling small aircraft with STOL (Short Take-Off and Landing) capability. This view is seen from the recently built Sir Steven Redgrave Bridge (named after the five-times Olympic rowing champion). Otherwise the scene is much the same as those opposite. The Royal Albert Dock is to the front and the King George V Dock is to the left. The Canary Wharf Tower and other tall Docklands buildings can be seen on the horizon.

Below: Taken in 2003, this photograph shows the Docklands Campus of the University of East London. The water in the foreground is the Royal Albert Dock. These four photographs sum up the changes that have occurred in this area – from being active docks, to dereliction, to the construction of a small but busy airport and now the development of a university campus.

Above: A District line train in Upney Station in the winter of 1964. The District line is part of the London Underground network and it commences in the east at Upminster and runs more or less parallel to the river from Essex and on through the centre of London. From Upminster to fairly close to the City, the District line track runs alongside the Fenchurch Street line.

Below: Steam locomotive en route to Southend, late 1950s. The Fenchurch Street to Southend and Shoeburyness train service stays fairly close to the river throughout its route. This photograph was taken just before the line was electrified and shows a 4-6-2 locomotive.

There were two very similar designs of locomotive working on this line prior to electrification in 1962. One was a class 4P, a three-cylinder design by Sir William Stainer and introduced in 1934. It was specifically produced for the London, Midland & Scottish Railway (LMSR), which operated this line prior to nationalisation. The second design was an 80xxx Standard Class 4 designed by R.A. Riddles for British Railways and introduced in 1951. The train photographed here is the BR Standard Class 4.

Opposite: Barking Station, 1964. This photograph was taken shortly after the station had been renovated. A key junction on the Fenchurch Street to Southend line is at Barking, where the line splits. The original line was via Tilbury and it reached Southend Central Station (as it is now known) in 1856. Due to the success of the railway, a more direct route between Barking and Southend was eventually opened in 1888, thereby avoiding the Tilbury loop.

The coming of the railway had a great impact upon Southend, as it cut the journey from London from one and a half days by sail to one and a half hours by train. Day trips to Southend from London were now a real possibility for people living in London and Essex; the concept of the day tripper had arrived. This social change was helped by the decision of the railway company to keep fares low.

Top: Barking Station, Christmas 1964. One of the trains that replaced the old steam locomotives is shown entering the station. In the background is a tall block of flats so typical of the 1960s.

Middle: Woolwich Ferry in centre of river, *c.*1970. The cranes belong to one of the Royal Docks. The Woolwich Ferry service, inaugurated in 1889, crosses the Thames between North and South Woolwich. At first it carried only passengers, but subsequently included vehicles. Up to the opening of the Dartford Tunnel (see chapter 4) it was the first realistic crossing of the Thames coming upriver. It is still operative today.

The Woolwich Ferry is also the junction between the North and South Circular roads. These two roads are closer to the centre of London than the M25 and can perhaps best be described as outer ring roads.

Bottom: A13, Newham Way, 1959. The A13 is a major trunk road going from London to Southend and running close to the Thames, and is referred to several times in later chapters. In 1959 it was possible to take a photograph through the car windscreen and have only one vehicle clearly visible – in this case a Ford V8 Pilot. Indeed, it appears that the V8 Pilot is actually parked on the road. The photograph also shows the slag heap associated with the Beckton Gasworks. This was sometimes called the 'Beckton Alp' and it is perhaps appropriate that for a time it was used as a dry-ski slope. Today the slag heap no longer exists and the area contains a large shopping complex as well as nearby housing estates.

Opposite page: Barking Carnival was (and still is) a major annual attraction in the town and usually a 'celebrity' was invited to open it. In 1974, the celebrity concerned was David Hamilton. For well over ten years, the local photography club (the Barking Photographic Society) mounted a special operation to cover the carnival in depth and, as a club member, for several years I walked the route photographing the floats and people watching the procession pass by. On this occasion I had the opportunity to get close to the guest celebrity. One of the themes in this book is how fashions have changed and this shot reflects a time when shirts had large collars and some had floral patterns.

CHAPTER 2
PEOPLE AND EVENTS IN BARKING AND DAGENHAM

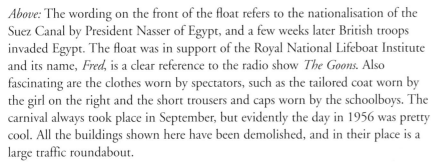

Above: The wording on the front of the float refers to the nationalisation of the Suez Canal by President Nasser of Egypt, and a few weeks later British troops invaded Egypt. The float was in support of the Royal National Lifeboat Institute and its name, *Fred*, is a clear reference to the radio show *The Goons*. Also fascinating are the clothes worn by spectators, such as the tailored coat worn by the girl on the right and the short trousers and caps worn by the schoolboys. The carnival always took place in September, but evidently the day in 1956 was pretty cool. All the buildings shown here have been demolished, and in their place is a large traffic roundabout.

Above right: The 'Kursaal Flyer', Barking Carnival, 1964. Carnival processions were held in many towns in this area and Barking's carnival generally included floats carrying the carnival queens from several different local boroughs. As noted several times in this book, the links between East London boroughs and Southend are considerable, and it was therefore an ideal opportunity for Southend to advertise itself. This it did by means of a carnival float, the so-called 'Kursaal Flyer'.

Right: Barking Carnival Queen, 1975. Behind the queen is Barking's then MP, Jo Richardson. They were seated on the stage in Barking Park during the presentation ceremony.

Above left: Norman Andrews, 1974. Norman, seen here taking photographs, was one of the leading members of the Barking Photographic Society and was always involved at carnival time. Cameras belonging to other club members are in the background, and their designs look archaic when seen from a distance of almost thirty years.

Above: Another member of the Barking Photographic Society, Bob Hayes, photographed at the Dagenham Town Show. This portrait emphasises one of the then current hairstyles and contrasts with other photographs in this chapter and elsewhere in the book.

Left: This group of people were listening to David Hamilton's speech at the 1974 Barking Carnival.

Barking Carnival, 1975. Walking the carnival route meant that there were many opportunities to take pictures of the spectators. If there was a gap between some of the floats, which invariably happened more than once during the course of the procession, then the photographer became a central source of interest and amusement.

Barking Carnival, 1975.

Opposite page, clockwise from top left:
Barking Carnival, 1974.

Carnival spectators in 1975.

Barking Carnival, 1979.

Barking Carnival spectator, 1978.

This page
Above: Cllr Joe Butler, 1965. Cllr Butler was the last mayor of the Essex Borough of Barking and this photograph was taken in the Council Chamber of Barking Town Hall. The mayor was the honorary president of the local photographic club, and several members used to take formal photographs of him – which is how I came to take the two photographs on this page.

Below: Alderman W.J. Bellamy, 1966. Alderman Bellamy was the first mayor of the London Borough of Barking and Dagenham, and this photograph was taken in Dagenham's Civic Centre. Previously Barking and Dagenham had been two separate Essex boroughs but they were merged following the reform of local government and the establishment of the Greater London Council. At the time it was not my intention to take photographs of the last mayor of the Essex Borough and the first mayor of the London Borough, but it just worked out that way.

Above: Frank Grainger, 1965. Mr Grainger was the headmaster of the County High School, Dagenham from 1954 until it was subsumed into the comprehensive system in July 1970. What relevance does this school have to a book on Essex Thames-side? After Ford Motor Company decided to construct its plant bordering the Thames at Dagenham a huge housing development known as the Becontree estate took place, providing homes for several thousand people. Within such a development it was necessary to have all kinds of services, including schools, one of which was this grammar school. Thus there is a direct link between this school and the development of riverside industry. The school was opened in September 1935 with sixty-eight pupils and Mr Grainger was the third headmaster (excluding the complications caused by the war-time evacuations of pupils to Ilfracombe in Devon and Southrepps in Norfolk). (Inevitably, having lived in Barking for so long and having attended this particular school during the 1950s, there is a strong element of autobiography in this chapter).

Left

Top: Also enjoying the summer sunshine near the end of term in 1959 are Mr Snape the school caretaker and Charlie the groundsman.

Middle: Three teachers, namely (from left) Mr Cooke, Miss Chittenden and Mr Rowlands, are seen here in 1959 enjoying the summer weather after all the examinations were completed. Hal Cooke was the school's geography teacher.

Bottom: The school's cricket first XI in 1958. Everyone wanted a copy of this photograph, and so, to use the modern parlance, it was a 'nice little earner'.

Left: Ray Church and Billy Bushnell, 1957. This photograph was taken while we were listening to records and, judging by the fact that Ray is playing 'air guitar', the music was almost certainly skiffle – most likely Lonnie Donegan. Most photographs of pupils at school such as these have been taken either by local newspaper photographers or by teachers. I believe that my photographs are almost unique as I was a sixth-former photographing fellow sixth-formers.

Below left: Ray Smith, 1958. Ray is taking a moment's breather while studying for A levels.

Below: V.H. Cackett's shop at Upney, Barking in 1962. Vic is just visible in the shop window. This photograph shows the old cigarette vending machines, which allowed cigarettes to be purchased at any time of the day. Their very nature meant that a purchase could be made by people of all ages and, once young people were stopped from buying cigarettes, these machines had to be withdrawn from uncontrolled locations such as this.

Telephone engineer, Barking, 1962. This photograph was taken in an estate built in the 1930s, and anyone wanting a telephone had to have the wiring specially installed. Therefore a pole like this was needed and the engineer is either installing a new telephone or repairing an existing line.

CHAPTER 3
INDUSTRIALISATION
BECKTON TO
SHELL HAVEN

Previous Page

Blue Circle cement works, 1969. This is perhaps the classic preconception of what an industrial site looks like, with lots of smoke pouring from chimneys. I deliberately chose to take this photograph, as a small group of us were at one time planning to have an exhibition on the theme of 'pollution' and I felt that this shot perfectly illustrated that idea. The cement works subsequently closed and, as will be apparent in the next chapter, its site duly became the Lakeside shopping centre. There was thus an element of pure chance that I photographed an industrial site that would in the course of the next few years close. However, as will be seen in this chapter, the industrial sector along the Thames no longer creates this sort of pollution – indeed there are now strict health regulations that govern the amount and type of pollutants which enter the atmosphere. This photograph was also taken from the (original) A13, which, as stated previously, runs close to the river throughout this part of Essex.

This page

Beckton Gasworks, 1959. This view is taken from the A13 looking along the Northern Outfall Sewer (known locally as the Sewer Bank). Following the 'Great Stink' of London during the summer of 1858, caused by the vile smell of sewage, Parliament passed an appropriate Act and the following year Joseph Bazalgette started to create a sewer network for the city. The Bank shown here is part of that network. Sir Joseph Bazalgette was responsible for many other projects in London, including the construction of the Victoria Embankment.

The ground below the Bank was split into parcels of land, which were called allotments, and were cultivated by local people to produce (mainly) fresh vegetables. The huts, shown in the lower part of this photograph, were used by the allotment-holders.

The industrial buildings shown above were part of the Beckton Gasworks, but they have now all been demolished. The Gasworks was opened in 1870 and was at the time the largest in Europe. This is one of the earliest industrial sites located on the Essex banks of the Thames. It was operated by the Gas Light and Coke Company, which owned some 450 acres of land fronting the Thames up to Barking Creek. The works continued in operation until 1969, its closure being caused by the introduction of natural gas.

Associated with Beckton Gasworks was a large slag heap known locally as 'Beckton Alp', which appears in a photograph in chapter 1. Nowadays, all that remains of the Gasworks are a few poles from its pier which are still standing in the river. Coal used in the manufacture of gas was brought to the Gasworks by river boats.

Barking Power Station, 1960. The power station is in the distance and was situated beside the river. This view was taken from the bridge by Upney Underground Station. Barking Power Station was one of the largest in Europe. It commenced operation in 1925 and ceased to generate electricity in 1981. It has since been demolished.

Two of the biggest power generation plants in Europe were therefore located beside the Thames within a few miles of each other. The fact that the Beckton Gasworks and Barking Power Station were situated beside the river is quite easy to explain – raw materials, particularly coal, could be brought by river transport to the respective sites. Subsequent photographs emphasise the importance of a riverside location for power station, oil refineries and other industrial activities.

This scene has since changed. The flats on the right have been re-styled and the space at the bottom of the hill has been filled by the construction of a large block of flats. One remarkable aspect of this photograph, noted several times during this book, is just how few vehicles there are. Only one van is moving and there are no more than three cars parked outside the flats.

This photograph shows a 1920s Ford Model T and a statue of Henry Ford, the founder of the Ford Motor Company. Henry Ford was born in Michigan in 1863 and in 1879 became an apprentice machinist with a firm in Detroit. He subsequently did various jobs and in 1891 joined the Edison Illuminating Company. He left that company in 1899 having already experimented with automobile engineering and eventually established the Ford Motor Company in 1903. The Model T was the car that made the company's fortune. The first one was sold in 1908 and production continued well into the 1920s. The price of this car was immensely attractive to the consumer and one reason for this was the development of mass production techniques, such as the moving production line, at Ford's Highlands Park plant in Detroit.

Some years ago the Rotary Club of Billericay Mayflower helped to organise a vintage car charity run, and associated with this was a raffle for which the Model T was the first prize. Because of the charity involvement, the club obtained special permission to take a series of photographs of the car at Ford's Dunton location. Since building the Dagenham plant, Ford have built other complexes within the general area of Essex Thames-side; this plant is actually situated in Basildon.

Left: This photograph of the Ford Logo is from an early model and is included because, without doubt, the most important industrial development on Essex Thames-side was the construction of the Ford Motor Plant in Dagenham in the early 1930s. As has already been noted, this in turn led to the building of a large infrastructure, including the County High School (chapter 2).

Right: Ford is an American company, and here is an early office block preserved in the Henry Ford Museum in Dearborn, on the edge of Detroit in Michigan. The Ford plants were in Detroit, which is sited on a river linking two of the Great Lakes, namely Erie and Huron, and this meant that the heavy raw materials needed in the construction of motor vehicles could be brought by waterborne transport.

Before the construction of the Dagenham plant, Ford had established a manufacturing base in Trafford Park near Manchester (its first production unit outside the US). However, the sale of its vehicles was so successful that a much larger plant was required and so Ford decided to build its Dagenham plant. This plant followed the same philosophy as the Detroit factories, as raw materials and finished products could be conveyed by river transport.

Above: Ford Motor works at Dagenham, 1993. This is clearly a highly industrialised area with many piers and jetties in the river, but the Ford works is quite distinct with its own dock. The sheer scale of the Ford plant can also be judged by simply looking at its roof area compared to all the other factories seen in this shot.

Below: The Kent bank of the river, directly opposite the Ford plant; the edge of its dock can be seen on the left side of this photograph (also taken in 1993). These photographs were taken on a flight from London City Airport and so the aircraft was still quite low as it passed along the Thames, even though visibility was reduced by the presence of low cloud.

This photograph was taken in 2003 from the PS (paddle steamer) *Waverley*, and the large structure on the left is Ford's old headquarters building. It clearly confirms that even today the river continues to provide an important transport corridor for the Ford Motor Company and the commentary on the *Waverley* stated that a ferry visited the Ford plant twice a day.

The plant was built on drained marshland and this led to some special problems, for instance 20,000 piles had to be driven into the earth. Henry Ford formally commenced construction work in 1929. It was a major project – it was the first factory in the south of England to have a blast furnace and its own power station was big enough to be able to supply a town of 180,000 people and, as is clearly shown from the photographs, it had its own dock by the river.

After its construction, Ford became the biggest employer in the Greater London area. The construction of the Ford plant in Dagenham and those in Detroit had several similarities. One intriguing consequence was that the development of the motor industry in and around Detroit led to a significant shift of population – many employees migrated from the south. The construction of the Dagenham plant also led to a similar shift in population. The need to house its employees led to the development of the Becontree (Dagenham) housing estate, which at the time was the biggest council (publicly owned) housing estate in the UK. As mentioned previously, this led to the need for an infrastructure, including schools.

It should be added that car manufacturing here ceased in 2003, and part of the plant is due for demolition. However, the Ford plant continues to operate and Ford is still a major employer within the whole of the Essex Thames-side area.

This car is a Model Y, otherwise known as a Ford 8 – '8' referring to its nominal 'horse power'. This particular car was produced in 1934 and its colour was described as electric blue. It is believed that the Model Y was only produced in this colour in 1934. My father owned the car, having purchased it in 1938, second hand, for £50. This photograph was taken in 1956.

This car went into production in August 1932 and was priced at £120. In 1933 nearly 33,000 were produced, taking Ford's market share to nearly one-fifth of all new cars sold. Subsequently, Ford's main competitors, Austin and Morris, also produced similar cars in order to meet the competition. It was a very successful project, which helped to make the Ford plant at Dagenham a commercial success. One reason for an 8hp engine was car taxation, which was related to a car's nominal 'horse power'.

The Ford 8 had a 933cc four-cylinder side-valve engine, a three-speed crash gearbox (i.e. no synchromesh) and a 6-volt battery. One effect of the low-voltage battery was that the headlights were very weak and it was no fun driving at night. On hot days it was possible to get fresh air by simply pushing the windscreen open! Finally, the windscreen wipers worked on pressure from the engine, which meant that as the car went faster or the load increased on the engine, e.g. going up hill, then the wipers slowed down. The only way to speed up the wipers was either to slow down or change gear, from (say) third to second. Travelling at a speed of 55mph was quite an experience, and the steep hills of Dartmoor proved too much for its small engine.

Opposite: Part of the Ford plant, seen from the old A13 in 1959. These buildings have been demolished as a result of the cessation of car manufacturing at Dagenham.

Also photographed from the old A13 in 1959, these towers (part of the Ford works) were demolished many years ago.

Right: The front of a 1934 Model Y – as explained earlier it was this car that helped to make the Dagenham plant a success. There is a muffler on the bonnet and this was used in winter to keep the water in the radiator from freezing. It is interesting that the word 'muffler' is used in the USA to describe a car's exhaust.

Below right: Wag Bennett's garage, 1959. This garage is close to the Ford works and is located between Dagenham and Rainham. When this photograph was taken it was actually sited on the A13; the garage is still in the same location but the A13 has been upgraded and moved. Wag Bennett is well known as a supplier of a wide range of car parts. The car on the forecourt is a Wolseley. Notice the old-fashioned Shell emblem on the petrol pump and the old oil dispensers on the left of the forecourt.

Below left: The cars in this photograph were participants in a vintage car rally, and here they are parked on the Esplanade at Westcliff-on-Sea. Behind the cars is the river Thames. These two models were both produced at Dagenham in the early post-war period. The model on the left is a 100E Prefect (also sold as an Anglia and subsequently a Popular), while the model on the right preceeded it and was sold as both an Anglia and a Popular. Both had four-cylinder engines, three-speed gearboxes (the 100E had synchromesh between 2 and 3) and both still 'enjoyed' windscreen wipers whose speed varied according to the pressure on the engine.

Above: Tilbury Fort and Power Station, 2003. This shows an intriguing contrast between the history of the river (Tilbury Fort) and its current (to use a pun) economic activity. The fort was built in the seventeenth century to act as one of the outer defences for London, to help thwart attacks from enemies such as the Dutch and the French. Its buildings are in the foreground and it is open to the public for viewing and for use as an exhibition centre. It was from near here that in 1588 Queen Elizabeth I spoke to the troops as the Spanish Armada approached, and it was in this speech that she stated: 'I know I have the body of a weak and feeble woman, but I have the heart and stomach of a king'.

Below: Tilbury Power Station, photographed from PS *Waverley*, 2003. The power station is located by the river with its own quay, thus enabling the raw materials used in the production of electricity to be delivered by water. While many power stations along the river have ceased to operate over the past couple of decades – such as Battersea, Bankside and Barking – the one at Tilbury continues to produce electricity for the National Grid.

Above: Tilbury Port, from the PS *Waverley*, 2003. Tilbury Docks were opened in 1886 and had the advantage over upriver docks in that ships could berth there at all times. They are now the only operational docks within the Port of London Authority, and are a major container port. In the past Tilbury was a major passenger port (London's gateway to the world) but this is no longer true. Photographs of two passenger ships at Tilbury are shown in chapter 5.

Below: Another view of Tilbury Docks from the PS *Waverley*, this time also showing the grain terminal. This is one of Britain's largest grain terminals, if not the largest.

Top: The Shell refinery near Corringham, 1960. As can be seen from the bottom photograph, most of these buildings have now been demolished.

The refinery, like many other industrial resources, was located right beside the river. The location is called Shell Haven, and I always thought that this name was due to the fact that the Shell Oil Company owned the refinery. This is not the case, however, as the name 'Shell Haven' appears on maps which pre-date by well over a century the construction and opening of the refinery.

The refinery has now been closed and is virtually dismantled. A consortium consisting of P&O (the Peninsula and Oriental Steam Navigation Company) and Shell (Shell UK Ltd) have submitted a planning application for the redevelopment of this site, to be called the London Gateway. The concept is to build a major container port, to be one of the largest in the country. This would be used for freight and general cargo and would involve the construction of a port, wharves, warehouses, a rail depot, new railway lines and major improvements to the A13, together with new or improved roads linking the A13 to the depot. The inquiry into this proposal started in February 2003. It should be noted that this plan has critics as well as supporters.

Middle: Shell refinery, 1960. The word 'Shell' can clearly be seen on one of the storage tanks. On the left side of the picture is a row of small cottages and it is perhaps surprising to find domestic homes so close to the refinery. These cottages were demolished many years ago – long before the recent demolition of the refinery.

Bottom: Shell refinery, 2003. By now most of the buildings have been demolished and further development of this site awaits the outcome of the London Gateway public inquiry.

Purfleet, 1969. This part of Essex, by the river, is much industrialised.

Oil storage tanks, Purfleet, 1969. Being located on the riverbank facilitates the delivery of raw material such as oil, and it is therefore not surprising that one element of the Essex bank is the number of oil storage depots and refineries.

CHAPTER 4
LAKESIDE SHOPPING CENTRE AND THE DARTFORD RIVER CROSSING

Previous page: Leaving the tunnel on the Essex side, 1963. The car in front is a Triumph Herald and this vehicle is visible in other photographs. The car on the right is a Rover.

Above: Road leading to the Dartford Tunnel, 1963. The tunnel had just been opened a week or so before this series of photographs was taken in 1963, and its newness is clearly evident from all the materials shown on the left-hand verge. The tall, slightly conical construction in the centre of the photograph is one of the ventilation shafts. This photograph was taken on the Kent side of the tunnel and the airshaft can still be seen above the tunnel entrance today.

The tunnel project had first been suggested in 1798 but was thereafter debated for many years. The idea gained impetus during the 1930s and a pilot tunnel was completed in 1938. However, work stopped in 1939 and did not recommence until 1957. The first tunnel was finally opened on 18 November 1963. The tunnel is 4,700 feet long and the initial estimates of some two million cars using it per year were soon proved to be an underestimate.

The opening of the tunnel meant being able to cross by road from Essex to Kent, and vice-versa, without going into east London and using either the Blackwall or Rotherhithe tunnels or, indeed, the Woolwich ferry. At this time motorways were only just starting to be opened in the UK and it was several decades before the tunnel became a part of the M25 London ring road. Living in Barking, I can confirm that the opening of the tunnel made getting to Kent much easier and subsequently facilitated the drive to Dover and hence the journey to the Continent.

Entrance to the newly opened Dartford Tunnel, 1963. At first the tunnel was a single bore with two-way traffic, as is clearly shown above. The leading car emerging from the tunnel is an MG saloon (Magnette). The slightly conical ventilation shaft is again clearly visible and this is still on the Kent side of the tunnel. The usage of the tunnel increased from four million vehicles per year in its first full year of operation to ten million by the early 1970s. Consequently, a second tunnel was required; work began on this in 1972 and it was opened to traffic in May 1980.

Tunnel entrance, 2003. This photograph (taken just before dusk) virtually duplicates the one on the left, albeit taken forty years later. The ventilation towers are still there, but the design of cars has changed considerably. However, the most remarkable feature is the way the Queen Elizabeth II Bridge now looms over the whole scene. As in 1963, this view is taken from the Kent side of the crossing. *(Photograph by Gill Thurman)*

The Queen Elizabeth II Bridge, 1998. This view of the bridge's pillars was taken during a traffic jam. It is a cable-stayed bridge and cost £184 million to build. The construction of the bridge started in August 1988 and was opened by the Queen in October 1991. The central span is 450 metres long and there are additional spans of 1,052 metres on the Essex side and 1,008 metres on the Kent side. At the time of its opening it was the longest bridge of its type in Europe and the third longest in the world.

Right: Even after the opening of the second bore, the traffic crossing the river at this point continued to increase substantially and it became an essential element in the M25, London's motorway ring road. This continuous growth led to the need for a further crossing and the Queen Elizabeth II Bridge was opened in 1991. It is seen here from a viewpoint on the Kent bank (photographed in 2003). The road itself is some 65 metres above the Thames. Since 1963 when the first tunnel was opened, the volume of traffic crossing the Thames at this point has risen from four million vehicles per year to an annual volume of some fifty million.

Below: This is another view of the bridge taken through a car windscreen in 2003. It shows clearly the cable stays.

Looking up at one of the towers of the bridge from the PS *Waverley* as it passes below in 2003. It is such a stunning creation that it deserves to be photographed from every angle and in every light condition.

Top: Looking towards the Queen Elizabeth II Bridge from the PS *Waverley,* 2003. The bridge is just visible in the murky light, but this view shows the way it crosses the river. Heavy road traffic can be seen on the bridge and could be jammed back from the pay booths. The tug is drawing a barge loaded with containers, while the tall tower behind the bridge is part of a power station.

Middle: Looking from Purfleet to the Kent side of the river, 1969. On the Essex side are some cranes and beside them is a moored ship. The tall, slightly conical construction is a ventilation shaft for the Dartford Tunnel. This view is looking south-east and the tall, smoking chimneys on the Kent bank are at Greenhithe. The dark buildings in the foreground are houses.

Bottom: I recently returned to this site to take a 'now' photograph. This was not possible, as the land in front of the dark houses in the previous picture is now (2003) being used for the construction of the high-speed rail link between London and the Channel Tunnel. However, there was a good viewpoint of the Queen Elizabeth II Bridge.

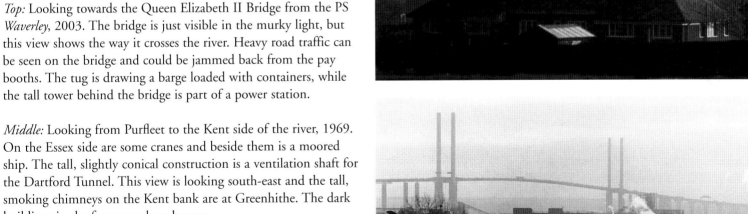

Blue Circle cement works, 1971. This photograph emphasises the smoking chimneys and the industrial nature of the site. The top photograph opposite shows that as well as smoking chimneys, this site also contained a very large quarry.

This photograph was taken on the approach road to the Dartford Tunnel long before that road was incorporated into the M25, the London orbital motorway. Indeed, this photograph was taken long before the M25, the second bore of the tunnel or the Queen Elizabeth II Bridge were constructed. Nowadays, looking across to the east from the M25, a view such as this encompasses the large warehouses of the Lakeside Retail Park and in the distance the Lakeside Shopping Centre.

There was one overwhelming impression when driving in the vicinity of the cement works. This was the simple fact that all the roofs of the private homes were covered in a white ash – presumably the fallout from these chimneys. While the smoking chimneys made good photographic material and were very illustrative of the impact of quarrying/manufacturing industry, the dangers of air pollution were recognised as long ago as 1956 with the enactment of the Clean Air Act.

Some years after this photograph was taken – in the late 1970s – the quarry and associated cement works were closed and replaced by the Lakeside development containing a shopping mall and retail park.

Above: Blue Circle cement works, 1969. This view of the Blue Circle cement works and associated quarry was taken from the (old) A13 road. The change from a quarry and cement works to a major retail site truly warrants the word dramatic.

Right: The Lakeside Shopping Centre, taken in 2003 from virtually the same place on the old A13 as the top photograph. All the industrial buildings have been demolished, although the lake remains. A fountain has been added, and the buildings on the left comprise a car park in the foreground and part of the shopping mall in the centre distance. Finally, trees have been planted to give a more pleasant overall impression. The whole complex is contained within the old quarry walls.

Above: Quarry floor of the Blue Circle cement works, 1969.

Below: Lakeside Shopping Centre, 2003. This view was taken from a lay-by on what used to be the A13 and therefore the view is also fairly complementary to the top photograph. The Queen Elizabeth II Bridge is visible in the distance, close to the dome at the centre of the shopping mall. One of the many outdoor car parks is shown in this photograph.

The shopping mall was opened in 1990, although the retail park, containing warehouse-style retailers, was in operation sometime before that. The statistics for Lakeside are impressive and give some idea of the sheer scale of its operation:

- 1.4 million square feet of retail space on a 120-acre site
- Over 320 shops, four major department stores and over thirty cafés and restaurants
- An average attendance of 500,000 visitors per week
- Parking space for 13,000 cars and 250 coaches.

CHAPTER 5
SHIPPING:
PURFLEET
TO CANVEY

Previous page: Cargo boat, 1963. This photograph was taken from the car park next to the Royal Hotel in Purfleet. In the foreground is a sail which appears to be part of a small raft. It is now very difficult to use this car park as a simple viewpoint due to the subsequent development of the site and the construction of a small hotel/travel lodge.

Lykes Lines was founded in 1906 as the Lykes Brothers Steamship Company and some years afterwards began operating entirely as a US flag carrier. During the 1920s and 1930s the company extended its services considerably, opening offices in Europe, including London. When this photograph was taken Lykes Lines was still an independent company, but in 1997 CP Ships (Canadian Pacific) acquired the company.

In addition to the vessels shown in this chapter, other river-going craft feature in many of the other chapters, such as the Woolwich Ferry, the Leigh-on-Sea fishing fleet and the yachts and sailing boats used for recreational and sporting purposes.

Above: RMS (Royal Mail Ship) *Arcadia*, moored at Tilbury in 1959. At one time Tilbury was an important passenger terminal (a 'gateway to the world'), although nowadays it is primarily a container port. Two 'period pieces' are the style of the lamp-posts and the small car – an Austin A35 – parked near the ship.

The RMS *Arcadia* was built in 1953 on the Clyde by John Brown & Company and operated by the P&O shipping line, entering service in February 1954. Her overall length was 721 feet and she was almost 91 feet at her widest point. Her gross displacement was 29,900 tons, which is only slightly larger than some of the ferries currently sailing between Dover and Calais. At that time she was the largest P&O passenger ship built on the river Clyde.

The *Arcadia*'s maiden journey was from Tilbury to Australia via the Suez Canal; she had been designed specifically for journeys to Australia and New Zealand, being one of a fleet of ships that were designed to travel between the UK and ports in Commonwealth nations. She continued to make regular journeys to Australia, interspersed with cruising from Britain, until the sheer speed of long-haul air travel completely changed the market.

This photograph was taken shortly after a major refit at Harland & Wolff in 1959. She continued in service with P&O on the Australia run, eventually concentrating on cruising, until 1979, when she sailed to a breaker's yard in Kaohsiung in Taiwan.

Above: MV (motor vessel) *Mikhail Lermontov*, a Russian cruise ship, photographed from Tilbury, *c*.1974. This ship had just set sail from the Tilbury pier, sailed upriver, turned, and was now on its way out to sea. In the background is the Kent coast, in the area between Gravesend and Northfleet. Like Essex, the Kent side of the river is also heavily industrialised. When this photograph was taken, Tilbury was an important departure point for Russian cruise liners, and on this particular trip the MV *Mikhail Lermontov* had just set off to sail to Leningrad (now St Petersburg).

The ship was built and launched in Wismar in 1972 in what was then East Germany and was owned by a Russian company, the Baltic Shipping Company. She was 155 metres long, nearly 24 metres wide and had a gross displacement of 20,351 tons. At first she sailed from Montreal to Tilbury and then on to Leningrad. By the 1980s she was spending six months in European waters and six months in Pacific waters.

On 6 February 1986 the *Mikhail Lermontov* left Sydney for a New Zealand cruise. She arrived in Wellington on 15 February and left later that day. On this particular trip there were 308 passengers, 330 crew and three pilots. She crossed from North Island to South Island via Cook Strait and arrived in Picton on Sunday 16 February. She left Picton at 1500 hours with the intention of travelling to Milford Sound via the West Coast. At 1737 hours she struck a reef between Cape Jackson and Walker Rock and was severely holed. All the passengers and crew (bar one) were rescued by a variety of craft. The ship subsequently sank.

The ship was named after Mikhail Lermontov, a Russian poet. He was born in 1814 and died in July 1841. His early death was the result of being shot dead in a duel by a fellow officer of the Russian Life Guard Hussars.

Below: A close-up of the MV *Mikhail Lermontov*, *c*.1974. In the background are some industrial buildings on the Kent coast.

Above: This three-masted sailing ship was a participant in the 1975 Tall Ships Race.

Below: A single Thames barge, 1975. This photograph was taken from a viewpoint on Canvey Island. The barge was participating in the parade of ships and other sailing vessels at the start of the Tall Ships Race. All the ships had left London Docks and were sailing downriver towards the open sea.

Thames barges were beautiful ships that were used for cargo until well into the second half of the twentieth century. They had a gross displacement of about 250 tons and were usually crewed by two men (and perhaps a boy). They were the largest vessels that could be handled by two men and were normally used for coastal trade, although they were also sailed to the Continent. They were flat bottomed, which meant they could sail well inland on rivers, and the masts could be dismantled so that they could sail under London bridges. One advantage in a port area such as London, with its high warehouses, was that its high topsail could catch any breezes above the warehouse roofs. This style of barge is known as a Spritsail barge, and it is so called because that is the name of the large diagonal boom that holds up the main central mainsail. This boom could also serve as a crane.

The peak time for their usage was from the nineteenth until well into the twentieth century. They continued to be used for the carriage of general cargo until after the Second World War, but thereafter their importance quickly declined. Nowadays, they are used for leisure purposes.

Above left: This ship was also photographed in 1975, as the tall ships sailed towards the open sea.

Above right: This tug is pulling a barge laden with containers containing the rubbish from central London. It is taken to a tip for disposal at the (appropriately named) Mucking, which is situated on the Essex bank of the Thames. It is a daily occurrence. This photograph was taken in 2003 from PS *Waverley*.

Below left: Cargo ship, taken in the early 1960s from the car park next to the Royal Hotel at Purfleet. It has a red star set on a blue funnel. There is a small tug at the rear of the ship.

Below right: These three cargo boats were photographed from Canvey Island in early 2003. The contrast with the small vessel in the left photograph is striking and demonstrates vividly the changes that have occurred in maritime transport over the past four decades. At least one of these ships is conveying containers, presumably to Tilbury, and another is operated by the Cobelfret line and is a roll-on roll-off ferry for commercial vehicles. Another Cobelfret ship was moored at the Ford Dock (see chapter 3). This shot also confirms that despite the closure of the upriver docks in central London, the Thames is still an important route for freight transport.

Tug boat, 1963, also taken from the car park beside the Royal Hotel at
Purfleet. On the opposite side of the river is the Kent bank. There
appears to be some kind of raft structure with a sail on the right.

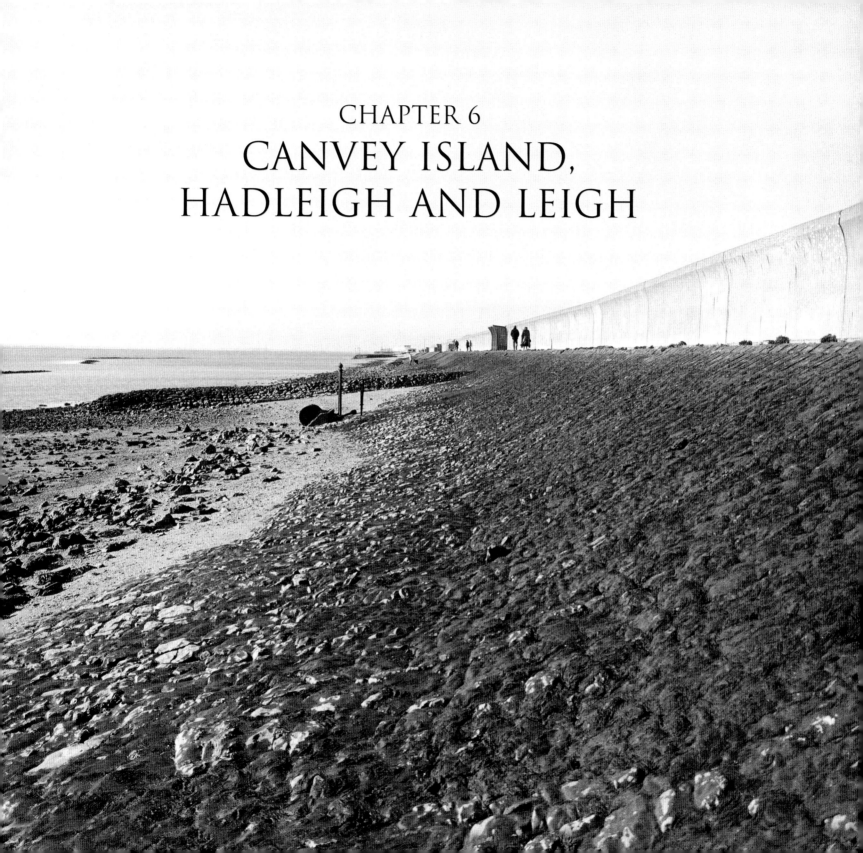

CHAPTER 6
CANVEY ISLAND, HADLEIGH AND LEIGH

Previous page: Sea wall, Canvey Island, 2003. The island is low lying and suffered badly in the terrible floods of 31 January 1953. The floods were the result of violent north-eastern gales which, combined with a surging high tide, led to severe flooding and loss of life. Hence the need for these high sea walls, which were photographed near to Chapman Sands Sailing Cub. While there was land here from earlier times, and Roman remains have been found, it was a Dutchman who helped to reclaim much of the island from the river in the 1620s.

It is at Canvey that the Essex bank begins to change. Part of Canvey Island is still industrial, but there are also parts that reflect leisure. Just downriver from Canvey is Leigh, with its shipping industry – see the next chapter – but thereafter the forthcoming photographs highlight both the residential nature and the various leisure activities of the greater Southend area.

Above: Canvey Island, 1961. Yachting is a favourite pastime on the Thames, and many more references will be made to sailing in later parts of the book. The Kent coast can be seen in the distance. At this point the river comes up to the sea wall, but a mile or so away, mud banks predominate at low tide, as shown opposite. The photographs of the Tall Ships were taken from this viewpoint.

Very close to Canvey Island is Two Tree Island, from where this
photograph was taken in 2003. The foreground is typical of this part of
the river when the tide is out and the large mud banks make sailing
treacherous. In the background are two cargo vessels as well as the Isle
of Grain Power Station.

Hadleigh Castle, 1960. There has been little change in this view over the past four decades. However, what was once described as an 'ancient monument' is now part of a fine country park and it is possible to walk into Southend via Leigh from the castle. John Constable, the famous landscape artist, painted Hadleigh Castle in the early part of the nineteenth century. The area where he lived in north Essex is now called 'Constable country' in today's tourist-speak!

As can be seen from this photograph, the castle stands on a hill and beyond it is some flat land, then the river and in the distance is Kent. It thus had a good position overlooking the Thames Estuary and was used in earlier times as a lookout to give advance warning of enemy ships approaching London. In this sense it served a similar purpose to the fort at Tilbury, shown earlier.

Hubert de Burgh built Hadleigh Castle in the early part of the thirteenth century. He was Chief Justiciar to King John (who reigned from 1199 to 1216) and then acted as regent when Henry III (1216-1272) first became monarch. Clearly he had a lot of power, but this came to an end following a disagreement with the young king.

The building continued to be developed, notably by Henry III and then by Edward III (1327-1377). At about this time it became the custom for the building to be granted to a tenant for life – among the tenants were three wives of Henry VIII (1509-1547), namely Catherine of Aragon, Anne of Cleves and Catherine Parr.

The building was sold by Edward VI (1547-1553) and subsequently fell into disrepair, mainly caused by the sale of the stones for other building purposes and landslides. Landslides continue to affect this part of the riverbank up to the present day.

Above: Marine Parade, Leigh-on-Sea, 1962. One interesting aspect, noted several times in this book, is the lack of cars on the road. The cars themselves are typical of the early 1960s and comprise an Austin Cambridge, a Bentley and a Ford Anglia (105E). The shadow in the foreground is mine.

Leigh has a strong fishing heritage, as is evident in the next two chapters. Indeed, it is said that the *Mayflower* called in here on its journey from Rotherhithe to Plymouth to take on victuals – including grain from Billericay. However, as the borough of Southend-on-Sea grew eastwards it eventually came to include Leigh, which became part of greater Southend in 1913. The houses shown above were built during the 1920s or early 1930s and have a prime position, as Marine Parade lies at the top of the river cliffs and from here there are good views over the river.

Marine Parade lies very close to Belton Way, from where the photographs on the left were taken.

Above: View from Belton Way West, Leigh, 1959. Beyond the car park and mudflats is Two Tree Island, and then beyond a further channel are Canvey Island, the Thames and some Kentish hills.

Below: Another view from Belton Way West, Leigh, 1959. Pictured from the same place as the top photograh, this photograph shows more of the view to the right, including both Two Tree Island and beyond that Canvey Island, although no industrial plant is visible on the island. There are, however, some lovely old cars in the car park.

Photographed in 1988 from Hadleigh Castle, this photograph shows a train on the Fenchurch Street to Southend and Shoeburyness railway line. Canvey Island is in the background, and the community is called Leigh Beck. The Thames is visible at the top of the photograph. As mentioned in chapter 1, the Fenchurch Street to Southend line also runs close to the river. This train is a later version of the rolling stock compared with the train in Barking Station on p.18. The British Rail logo is just visible on the front of the engine. Before nationalisation in 1947, this line was operated by the LMS railway.

This photograph was taken in 2003 from Hadleigh Castle. In the background is some of the industrial plant on Canvey Island. A comparison with the 1959 photographs suggests that this industrialisation has occurred since then, and as will be apparent from a subsequent photograph, its location by the river is important. The current version of the rolling stock used on the Fenchurch Street to Southend line is described more fully in chapter 9.

Right: Customers of the Crooked Billet pub in Old Leigh basking in the sun on a Sunday afternoon in 2002. This is a major social change as it is only recently that the licensing laws were changed to allow pubs to open during Sunday afternoon – only a few years ago their hours were 12 (noon) to 2 p.m. and from 7 p.m. to 10.30 p.m. Another striking change is that the umbrella bears the name 'Grolsch', a Dutch lager. In 1960, when the first photographs in this book were taken, lager accounted for only 1 per cent of beer sales, while in 2002 lager accounted for over 65 per cent of the market.

Leigh Regatta, 1976. It is probable that the rowing boat with five
oarsmen belonged to the local Sea Scouts.

Above: This view from Two Tree Island towards the Essex 'coast' was taken in 2003, and shows just how far the tide recedes. On the horizon is the Essex coast from Chalkwell, via Westcliff to Southend-on-Sea. In the distance can be seen the very tall block of flats near the Westcliff Hotel, while the centre of Southend lies at the end of the hill, in the centre of the photograph. It is interesting to see the yachts standing on their keels when the tide is out.

Left: A tanker unloading at a plant on Canvey Island, 2003. This scene was taken from the PS *Waverley* and, together with the photographs above and opposite, shows again the wide variety of vessels that use the river.

CHAPTER 7
LEIGH-ON-SEA
FISHING FLEET

Previous page: Some of Leigh's fishing fleet, 1960. The nearest boat to the camera is the *Heather Pam*, and then moving away from the camera are the *Boy David*, *Rainbow* and *Endeavour*. This is the earliest photograph of these boats, and it is interesting to note that some of these boats appear in later photographs.

A group of six boats took part in the Dunkirk evacuation at the end of May 1940. The *Endeavour* was one of these and is now the subject of a major restoration project.

Some land can just be seen on the horizon and this is the County of Kent. One aspect of this part of the river is the large tidal effect that leads to the exposed mud banks. It is this effect which allowed for the construction of the very long pier at Southend as described in a later chapter. The tidal effect also limits the time in which the fleet can actually sail and return to port. The watercourse shown here is Leigh Creek.

Above: Leigh-on-Sea, 1973. Among the boats photographed on this occasion are the *Boy David*, *Rainbow* and the *Ceresta*. Leigh has a seafaring history going back many centuries and today the village retains this nautical heritage in the form of its fishing fleet. It specialises in shellfish and is well known for its 'cockle sheds' (see next chapter). In many ways it seems surprising to find such a fishing village on a busy river with ocean-going ships serving so many industrial sites. This view shows some fishing boats, while part of old Leigh village can be seen on the foreshore.

Below: Leigh Creek looking upriver, 1973. One of the problems facing the fishermen is that these channels move over time and the existing ones can silt up. It is essential that the channels continue to exist near the foreshore so that the catches can be landed. This means that every now and then dredging operations become vitally important for Leigh's continued existence as a fishing port. The situation now (2003) is that the silting is so bad that if boats sail to the end of this creek, it may be some weeks before the tide is such that they are able to return to the centre of Leigh.

The appearance of so many gulls just adds to the atmosphere of the occasion. The boat is the *Ranger* and was photographed in 1973. I photographed this fishing boat on many occasions over several years and more details of it are given overleaf. The small strip of land in the background is Two Tree Island, and the other boats are signs of recreational sailing.

Above: Leigh, 1988. The boat at the front is the *Almar* (LO 348); moving right and in the distance is the *Letitia* (LO 422) which is very low in the water, thus indicating that it is full of cockles. Nowadays, cockle fishing is only allowed for six months of the year and then only for a few days a week during the fishing season. There were no engines in the fishing boats until 1921, and one of the last remaining boats was the much smaller white vessel on the right, which was owned by the Livermore family. The first engines were difficult and they had to be warmed by blowlamps before they would ignite.

All these boats have the letters LO, which stand for London, as Leigh does not have its own registration letters.

Below: Leigh, 1988. LO 422, the *Letitia*, was the Dench boat, which is no longer used for fishing. A contrast between this and the other boats so far is that it has more equipment above deck. The reason for the plank on the side of the boat will be evident in the next chapter. The older boats had their wheelhouses to the rear, but the more modern designs have them to the front. The tall chimney seen on the horizon is at the Isle of Grain Power Station in Kent.

Above: Leigh, 1960. Two traditional boats berthed on the mudflats. I have photographed LO 92 on several occasions, and in some other photographs it is shown as *Ranger II.* The second boat in this photograph is LO 501, the *Vanguard,* which was operated by Harvey's, the owners of the No.1 cockle shed.

At the time of this photograph the *Ranger* was owned by Tony Meddle, and then in 1967 it was leased to the MAFF (Ministry of Agriculture, Fisheries and Food) to undertake trials regarding a new method of fishing. Up to that date the collection of cockles from the cockle beds had been done by hand, but the purpose of the trials was to test a new form of fishing known as 'suction dredging'. The trials proved successful and this method duly became the normal method of collecting cockles. After the tests the *Ranger* was sold and subsequently used for whitebait fishing.

The mudflat shown beyond the two boats is known as 'Gasboy Gut', and this has moved considerably since this photograph was taken. The mudflat has moved nearer to the foreshore and the creek has gradually silted up. Such movement is only evident when looking at comparable photographs over a period of time such as this, that is, four decades. The land beyond the mudflats is Two Tree Island.

Below: Leigh, 1972. Another view of LO 92, now called *Ranger II,* with the Gasboy Gut mudflat behind it. A dock has now been built in the foreground.

Above: Leigh, 2002. The Meddle family owned *Ranger II*, and another long-established Leigh family, the Osbornes, owns the *Renown*. It is interesting to compare this photograph with the previous one. Behind the *Renown* is the mudflat Gasboy Gut and it has moved nearer to the hard standing. Furthermore, both shots were taken at low tide and Leigh Creek has clearly silted up. The hard standing is now such that people can comfortably walk on it. In the background is Two Tree Island. The *Renown* is a famous name in Leigh, as an earlier boat of the name was lost in the Dunkirk evacuation of 1940. This *Renown* is a modern vessel and the differences in design are strikingly obvious.

Above right: The two vessels on the right are both modern fishing boats and so are very different from the old LO 92 *Ranger*. The boat above is the *Freya*, taken in 2003, which clearly shows the amount of equipment used in a modern fishing vessel. The front of *Freya's* skiff is on the left, while behind it is a vessel visiting from another port.

One of the changes that have occurred over the past decades is that the boats themselves have become considerably more expensive, from a few thousand pounds in the past to approaching £250,000 nowadays. This is due to several reasons: the cost of raw materials and manufacturing, the introduction of modern fishing equipment and the advent of electronic navigational aids.

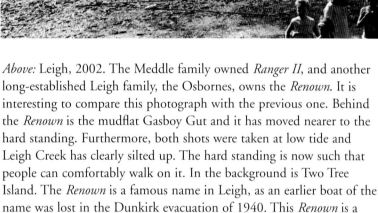

The *Liberator*, taken in 2003, showing from a different angle the equipment used on a modern fishing boat plus a view of its open hold. The wheelhouses are at the front so as to give space to the modern suction dredging equipment.

Leigh, 1964.

Leigh, 1964. The two people are walking on the Meddle hard. Since
then new docks have been constructed. This is a westward view towards
Hadleigh and London. The river scene at Leigh at Sunset is, for me,
magical.

CHAPTER 8
LEIGH-ON-SEA: LANDING AND SELLING THE FISH

Previous page: Leigh, 1988. This shows Dave Brinkley unloading fish from the *Theodore.* By 1988, the wheelhouse was at the front of the boat but I have another photograph not used in this book which shows that some six years earlier the wheelhouse had been at the rear of the vessel. This change had taken place to enable more modern equipment to be incorporated into the boat.

I was lucky to get this sequence of photographs for several reasons. Fishing only occurs for a few days per week and for a few weeks per year due to the need to preserve stocks. Furthermore, the catch can only be landed when the tide is favourable. However, the most fortuitous aspect was to record the fishermen landing the catch, by a method which had been used for many centuries. The shellfish were put into boxes or pails and then carried on shore by the use of yokes. It was not unknown for a new fisherman to miss his footing on the plank and fall into the water. However, a few years after taking this sequence of photographs this centuries-old practice no longer existed and today everything is now motorised.

Above: Leigh, 1988. Dave Brinkley is descending from the boat on the left (*Letitia*) while a second boat, LO 58 (*Katherine* with Les Snell on board) is also unloading its catch. LO 58 is clearly a more modern vessel than some of the other boats featured in this book, such as LO 92. It is also interesting to see the gulls hovering around the boats while they unload their fish. Gulls are scavengers and are no doubt looking for any morsels to eat.

Below: Leigh, 1988. This is the Dell-owned *Katherine*; Colin Philpott remains on the boat, Garry Dench is on the plank and Steve Dell waits to re-board.

Above: Leigh, 1988. This is the Dench boat *Letitia*, with Roger Brooks carrying the pails, while Kenny Kerry remains on board.

Below: Leigh, 1988. In this scene there are two men using yokes while two other men (Les Snell and Colin Philpott) are on board putting the fish into pails. On shore a small truck is used to carry the fish to huts where they are cooked and prepared for sale to either wholesalers or the general public. It is one of the traditions of the industry that all the fishermen have nicknames, and the young man standing beside the truck is known, for instance, as 'What, What'. These trucks are not used anymore as everything is automated.

Above: Leigh, 1988. Steve Dell is using the yoke, while Garry Dench is on the right edge of the picture. Les Snell and Colin Philpott are on the boat.

Below: Leigh, 1988. Derek Cotgrove is on the boat. This view, like other photographs in this sequence, shows the above-deck equipment used on a fishing boat in 1988.

Opposite: Leigh, 1973. After landing their catch, the fishermen had to cross this stretch of 'beach' to reach the cockle huts shown on page 82. This view also shows the 'old' paths to the cockle sheds.

Among the boats moored in this photograph are the *Navigator, Letitia, Boy David* and *Liberator.* The trials for suction dredging were carried out in 1967/68 and the relevant equipment started to be installed in 1969. This photograph was taken some four years later and it is interesting to note that some of the boats carried the new gear while others were unchanged.

This scene contrasts with the photograph opposite; by 2003 the sheds had become much larger. The one being extended at the moment is owned by Osborne Bros, while the other large shed is Meddle's. The lone fishing boat is *Ranger II*.

Leigh, 1973. The shed in the front of this photograph was owned by S. Meddle, and then comes the 'noted No.3' shed (see overleaf). The next two sheds were owned by F.A. Emery (now owned by George Dell) and then near where the van is parked is a much smaller shed that was a boat repair yard. Continuing along the line, the next shed was owned by Bridge and Osborne and specialised in whitebait. Beyond that were sheds owned by the Coral Seafood Company, then another Meddle shed and finally (No.15) one owned by C&A Osborne.

However, since 1973 times have changed. As shown opposite, the sheds have become bigger for various reasons, and two of the families (Osbornes and Meddles) have joined together to jointly own Thameside Fisheries.

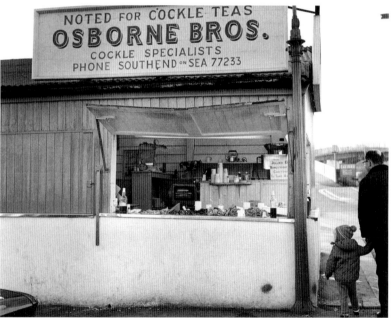

Opposite page, clockwise from top left:
Leigh, 1973. The cockle sheds are one aspect of the fishing trade in Leigh that are well known to townspeople and visitors alike. The previous photographs showed the closeness of these sheds to the river (Leigh Creek). They are on the edge of the village and are the places where the shellfish is cooked.

This photograph shows the 'shop front' of one of the sheds. As can be seen from the signs, a wide variety of fish is on sale, including cockles, mussels, whelks and eels as well as local shrimps caught daily. Generally speaking, the fish is sold for cooking and consumption at home, but it is also possible to buy small plates of fish, normally cockles, to eat on site, standing up outside the shed. One of these small plates is visible to the right-hand side of the shed counter.

The Osborne family owns this shed, and the lady looking after the fish is Glad West, a member of that family.

Leigh, 1973. This is another view of the same shed owned by W.H. Osborne. The Osbornes are one of the Leigh families that have been involved in the fishing industry for generations. The large placard confirms all the different types of fish on sale. The lady on the left, Glad West, is selling the fish, while the man on the right, with the then fashionable flared jeans, is a customer.

Leigh, 1973. The lady on the right, who is serving in the café, is Florrie Lawrence, while the lady on the left is a customer. One of the traditional measures for buying shellfish to take away has been the pint and half-pint. In this case the server has two small plates in her hand which strongly suggests that the customer is buying a small portion of shellfish for eating in the café, perhaps with a cup of tea.

Leigh, 1973. This building is in the centre of old Leigh and is both a café and a stall selling sea fish to passers-by for either eating at home or by the stall. Quite clearly a speciality of this café, owned by the Osbornes, is its cockle teas.

Chapter 6 contains a photograph of people drinking in front of the Crooked Billet pub; behind the drinkers this café is clearly visible. Very little has changed in the intervening decades except that the name board above the café has a new design. A comparison of the two boards leads to the immediate conclusion that the style of typefaces used in 1973 now looks very dated.

This page: Leigh, 1964. A view back to the old fishing village; the quay with the crane was once full of cottages. This photograph was taken before suction dredging and hence there are no flexible hoses etc. The *Boy David* is in the front and then the *Rainbow*. This quiet scene was taken at dusk.

Leigh, 1973. A final view, showing one of the planks, and then beyond that is the village of Leigh. The boats are, from right to left: the *Theodore*, *Reliance* and the *Ranger*. The 'beach' was often strewn with shells from some of the fish. One by-product of this industry has been the purchase of shells by local clubs to provide a good walking surface on particularly muddy paths in winter. It is rather strange playing golf accompanied by the aroma of shellfish!

As seen, there have been some major capital investments made during the period covered by these photographs – new boats, modern fishing equipment, new hards and extensions to the sheds. All of this is indicative that this small fishing enclave is continuing to prosper.

CHAPTER 9
CHALKWELL AND
WESTCLIFF-ON-SEA

Previous page: Chalkwell, 1965. This yacht may imply that it had been hired by a group who wanted to enjoy the pleasures of sailing under canvas. However, on this occasion it would appear that their luck (and the tide) ran out as there are two people in the water pushing the vessel. The position of the sails is known as a gaff rig.

Chalkwell developed at the beginning of the twentieth century, when Southend-on-Sea gradually extended westwards, firstly to Westcliff-on-Sea and then on to Chalkwell. It contains many fine houses from the first few decades of that period and it is possible to walk beside the river from Old Leigh via Chalkwell as far as Thorpe Bay.

Chapters 9, 10 and 11 continue the coastline towards the mouth of the river, being concerned with Chalkwell, Westcliff-on-Sea, Southend-on-Sea and Thorpe Bay. Leigh and all these other places are really parts of the same conurbation that comprise the unitary authority known as Southend-on-Sea. This conurbation has a population of over 175,000 people and while the communities on the river upstream from Leigh towards London were, and are, highly industrial, the downstream from Leigh has invariably been leisure based.

Top: A train on the track by the sea between Chalkwell and Leigh Stations, 1955. Full details of the different locomotives used on this line were given in Chapter 1; on balance this is thought to be a Stainer-designed class 4P.

Middle: A train on the track between Chalkwell and Leigh Stations, 2003. These two photographs summarise the changes that have occurred on this line over almost fifty years, from steam to very modern Electrostar trains. Other photographs of trains using the Fenchurch to Southend line are shown in chapters 1 and 6.

Bottom: A train on the track between Chalkwell and Leigh, 2003. The trains on this line are now run by a company known as 'c2c', part of the National Express group of companies. For many years this service – between Fenchurch Street and Southend – was known as the 'misery line' because of the quality (or more accurately lack of it) of its rolling stock and track. In recent years c2c has invested some £400 million in improving the service. Part of this improvement is the introduction of seventy-four new Electrostar trains.

As can be clearly seen, at this point the track runs right beside the river. The original plan of the railway company in the 1850s was that the track should continue beside the river right up to the centre of Southend, but this was opposed by Southend residents. The original proposals were duly changed as a result of their representations, made while the Bill establishing this railway was passing through the Houses of Parliament. They did not want their access and enjoyment of the river frontage to be spoilt by the construction of the railway. Consequently, when the line was built the track moved inland and entered Southend at what is now Southend Central Station.

NIMBY is a phrase that has evolved over the past few years and stands for 'Not In My Back Yard'. This applies to people who protest at new developments because they spoil the amenity in the vicinity of their home. However, the opposition to the proposal that the railway should run alongside the river shore shows that NIMBY is not a new occurrence!

Above left: This kiosk selling ice cream is located on the seafront at Westcliff. The photograph was taken on an August bank holiday in the early 1970s. The clothes are very formal – a man who has just bought ice cream is wearing a tie and some of the younger boys have tailored short trousers.

Above right: Westcliff gardens one August bank holiday, about 1970. A classic scene of people relaxing in the afternoon sun, sitting in deckchairs hired from the local council.

Below left: Rossi's Restaurant, Westcliff, 1963. Rossi's ice cream is very much a Southend speciality and this restaurant is on the seafront at Westcliff and a popular stopping off spot as people arrive in Southend for their day or afternoon visits. Our family often made a day trip to Southend which was only thirty-five miles from Barking; thousands of other families living in east London or in the (then) Essex boroughs like Barking made a similar trip. This behaviour pattern continues to the present day – even in the middle of winter, provided the weather is good, the car parks on Southend front are full by the early afternoon.

Below right: Rossi's Restaurant, 2003. A number of changes are immediately apparent, the most important of which is the construction of the Cliffs Pavilion. Discussions about the possibility of a Cliffs Pavilion had been underway for many years, but eventually the project came to fulfilment in 1964, when Sir Bernard Miles formally opened it. Part of the pavilion can be seen at the top of the cliffs on the right, and there is an entrance close to Rossi's Restaurant at street level. The large trees on the left of the 1963 view have been cut down, and there are a few intriguing changes in the houses behind the restaurant.

Left: The large stone column is called the Crowstone, and it stands on Chalkwell beach. Its purpose was to mark the eastern end of the City of London's jurisdiction over the river, but all this came to an end with the establishment of the Port of London Authority in 1908. At the time this view was taken in 2003 the tide was out, which meant that people could walk up to the Crowstone. At high tides the stone is in the water, as is the groyne, which is the other main feature shown here. Groynes are typical features of many seaside areas in Britain, and their purpose is to safeguard the beach and prevent erosion and drifting. I was intrigued to find that one source of this word is from the late Latin meaning 'pig's snout'.

Below: Children playing on the beach in early spring sunshine, 2003. It just shows how, in the first hint of a warmish sunny day, people still come to Westcliff to play on the beach. But it is the children's clothes that make such a contrast to the 1970 scenes. Nowadays, the vogue is to have 'designer gear' and wear full-length trousers at whatever young age.

Above: Restaurants under the arches at Westcliff in 2002. People are eating out of doors, their dress is casual, and the man with the ice cream is in shorts. There are many Italian restaurants – Mamma Mia, Flying Pasta and Piccolo – in the street above the arches. One change over the past decades is the ever-greater willingness to try foreign food, as witnessed by the Italian restaurants in this scene. The fact that there are so many restaurants, Italian and otherwise, confirms that they must have enough customers to survive.

Below: Another view of these restaurants in Palmeira Terrace, taken in winter sunshine, 2003. Awnings and windbreaks protect diners from any 'winter nip in the air'. The conclusion to be drawn from these two photographs is that deep down, given the right climate, the British would love to be a café society. It is all so different from the 1940s. Admittedly, behaviour was then constrained by post-war austerity, food and petrol rationing, but nevertheless since then there have been some huge social changes, including much less formal wear and much more eating away from home. In 1965, there were 3,500 restaurants licensed for the sale of alcoholic drinks with meals (as opposed to hotel and public houses) in England and Wales; by 1998 this figure was 21,000. These two photographs certainly emphasise how people like to eat out of doors.

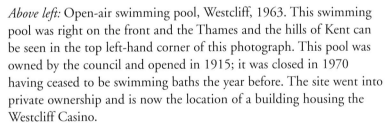

Above left: Open-air swimming pool, Westcliff, 1963. This swimming pool was right on the front and the Thames and the hills of Kent can be seen in the top left-hand corner of this photograph. This pool was owned by the council and opened in 1915; it was closed in 1970 having ceased to be swimming baths the year before. The site went into private ownership and is now the location of a building housing the Westcliff Casino.

Above right: Another view taken at Westcliff's open-air swimming pool in 1963.

Right: Looking towards Southend Pier, 1961. This view is taken from the Westcliff side and shows the pier and one of its electric trains in the background. In the foreground are two traditional deckchairs.

Previous page
Above left: Steps leading from the seafront to the top of the cliffs and the pavilion, Westcliff, 1963.

Above right: Stairs, Westcliff, 2003. These steps still remain, but during the intervening forty years there have been some changes. The lights are modern, the front of the steps have been retiled and much of the greenery has been reduced. Most notably some tall trees have been removed, and the overall impression is of a more spacious aspect.

Below left: Westcliff Hotel, 1963.

Below right: Westcliff Hotel, 2003, taken from virtually the same angle as the 1963 view. As the building to the right of the main hotel is now painted white, it would lead to the conclusion that the hotel has expanded over the intervening four decades. It is also interesting to reflect that of the three original leading seafront hotels, only the Westcliff is still operating.

This Page
Above: Photographed in 2003, this is one of many beautiful houses that line the cliff-top road in Westcliff-on-Sea. As Southend developed during the latter part of the nineteenth century, it spread both westwards and eastwards along the river. The first development was westwards and led to the development of the suburb of Westcliff. There are many fine houses and avenues in this area near to the centre of Southend-on-Sea.

Below: These Art Deco flats are on the Esplanade at Westcliff and were photographed in 2003. From these flats it is a short walk into the centre of Southend.

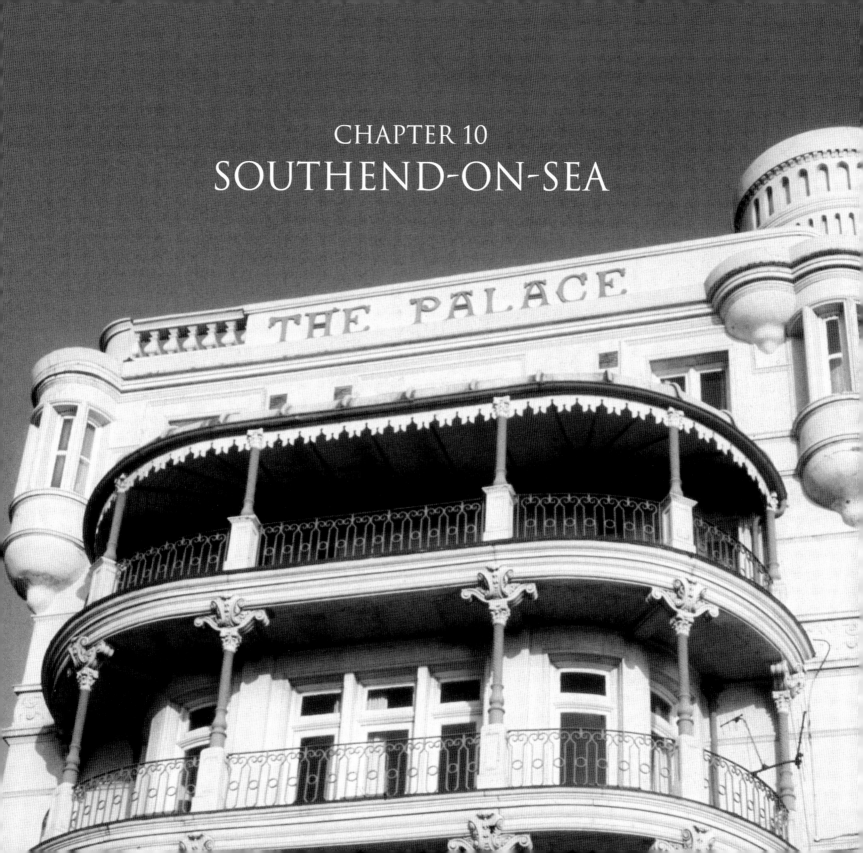

CHAPTER 10
SOUTHEND-ON-SEA

Previous page: The Palace Hotel could be said to epitomise the elegance of the Edwardian period (pre-1914) and perhaps the inter-war years. This view of the balconies on the front of the hotel, taken in the late 1960s, shows some of the fine ironwork just above its entrance.

The hotel was opened in 1900 and was originally called the Metropole but was shortly renamed the Palace. It had 100 bedrooms and was truly a grand hotel, being described during its heyday (pre-1914 and the inter-war period) as the most prestigious hotel in the south east of England. During the two world wars it became a military hospital, its name during the First World War being Queen Mary's Naval Hospital. Attempts were made to recapture its former glory days after 1945, but social circumstances had changed and in 1958 it was put up for sale by auction. Among those who arrived to make a bid were Sir Isaac Walton, Sir Billy Butlin – both in their Rolls Royce cars – and a local Southend councillor and businessman, Motel Burstin, who arrived by bicycle. In the event, Mr Burstin was successful and his vision was to house the elderly in comfortable surroundings with all mod-con apartments. This vision became a reality and for many years the Palace Hotel performed that role.

A change in the needs of the local community led to many of the apartments being used by the local authority to house people in need. The hotel remained in the Burstin family until 2000 when it was sold to new owners. It continues to meet local social needs, but its future direction is currently unknown. One thought is that it might become a conference centre. What is true, however, is that it is a stunning Edwardian building whose situation commands superb views over the Thames Estuary and which itself can be seen from miles away.

Above left: Palace Hotel, Southend, early 1960s. The hotel stands on the brow of Pier Hill and therefore has a superb location within Southend. In the foreground is a row of shops, most of which are small restaurants with many having fish and chips as a speciality. Among the parked cars is a Triumph Herald and on the road is a bubble car. Evidence that this photograph was taken on one of the first fine weekends in spring is that most people are in winter coats, although the man crossing the road is in a suit.

A comparison with the top photograph opposite shows that buildings have vanished. Firstly, the large brick building with ironwork balconies on its first floor was called the Pier Hill Buildings and these were constructed about the end of the nineteenth century. They were demolished in the 1970s. Behind them is a white building with a pillared portico that housed an aquarium. This was presumably knocked down at the same time. Further changes are noted opposite.

Above right: The lounges of the Palace Hotel, photographed in the late 1960s. On the lower right corner are the letters 'Ro', a reference to Rossi's ice cream, for so long a Southend favourite. Some of the hotel residents can be seen relaxing in the lounge and enjoying the late winter or early spring sunshine.

Above: Palace Hotel, 2000. The size and elegance of this Edwardian building can be directly compared to the opposite left-hand photograph. In addition to the changes noted opposite, there have been others during the four-decade interim. The design of the white restaurant has altered, as have the style of cars and lamp-posts, while the decorative illuminations remain. The square archway on the right was the entrance to the pier and was situated on the bridge across the road. This no longer exists and in its place is a new entrance (see later photographs in this chapter). In 1960, the bridge was made of brick but had become a concrete edifice by the end of the century. However, this has also been recently demolished and replaced by another bridge. Through all this change, the Palace Hotel continues to dominate the landscape.

Below: Palace Hotel, early 1960s. The trees are just breaking into leaf and so it is likely that this photograph was taken on one of the first fine spring weekends of that year. Many changes have taken place since this photograph was taken, not least in the design of the cars – among the parked cars are a Ford Popular and an Anglia 105E, while an Austin A30 is being driven along the road.

It was the growth of railways in the nineteenth century that had led to the development of Southend-on-Sea as a major seaside resort for both day trippers and longer holidays. It is ironic that it was another leap in transport – the advent of turboprop (such as the Vickers Viscount shown later in this chapter) and jet aircraft – which changed that again. Allied to cheap package holidays, this much faster form of transport led to the growth of Spanish resorts at the expense of Southend and other English seaside resorts. Such a change in holiday patterns was bound to be reflected in the fortunes of this hotel and led to its change of use.

Above: Southend Pier, *c.*1970. This is the end of the pier, taken from Thorpe Bay, at sunset. The main buildings are on the left and then in the centre is an additional building which housed the lifeboat. A slipway coming from the lifeboat house down to the water can be seen. To the right of the photograph is one of the pier's electric trains.

The first pier at Southend was opened in 1830, while the current pier which replaced it was designed by Sir James Brunlees and opened in 1889. The pier is over 1.25 miles long and is certainly the longest in the country. Various claims have stated that it is the longest pleasure pier in the world, or the longest in Europe, or the longest in the Commonwealth. What made the project feasible were the tides; at low tide it is possible to walk around the base of the pier head. Later photographs in this chapter show this effect.

The pier was built for a very practical reason: to overcome the drawbacks of the low tides. It meant that fairly substantial cargo and passengers boats could dock at the pier head. Among the destinations for ships calling at the pier were London, Ramsgate and Margate. Its heyday for passengers could well have been the later 1940s, when the numbers passing through the pier were between three and five million people per year. The pier head was destroyed by fire on 29 July 1976.

Below: Taken in 2000, this photograph shows the end of Southend Pier almost a quarter of a century after the fire and provides a good comparison to the view above. There are no buildings on the pier head. When the tide retreats, there is good space for dog walking! Behind the pier is the Isle of Grain Power Station on the Kent side of the river.

Above: This shows part of the entrance and part of the bridge that used to link Pier Hill with Southend Pier. This has now been demolished as part of the scheme to rebuild the entrance to the pier. This photograph was taken in the late 1960s.

Below: A new entrance to the pier was built in 2003 and this photograph was taken shortly after it was opened to the public. The pier can be seen in the distant haze and on the left is a wooden galleon open to the public. This entrance replaced the one shown in the above photograph and is part of the process of rejuvenating the pier.

Above: Southend Pier looking very forlorn in 2000. Since this photograph was taken work has been undertaken to improve the pier. A photograph of the new entrance has already been included and a view of the new pier head appears later in this chapter. The children's playground, 'Adventure Island', with its various fairground rides, is in the foreground of the picture.

Below: Southend's pier is over a mile and a quarter in length and one way of reaching the pier head is to walk – as two people are doing in the photograph on the opposite page. Another way is to use the pier's own train – a feature unique to Southend. This view shows the length of the train, which allows those unable or unwilling to walk to reach the pier head. River ships (such as the PS *Waverley*) still occasionally call at the pier head and this train facilitates access to and from such boats.

Below left: A close-up of the pier train, taken in 2003, showing both the cab and driver. In the background are some of Southend's buildings including, most noticeably, the Palace Hotel.

Opposite: A classic view looking along the pier, taken in hazy winter sunshine in early 2003. The pier head is in the distance, and a comparison with the view above shows how construction work has changed its outline. Among the current end-of-pier attractions is a café serving fish and chips.

A fisherman collects bait under the pier head in 1965.

Another view of the fisherman collecting bait in 1965 taken from the end of Southend Pier. It shows just how far the tide recedes and why it was possible to build a long pier as well as why a long pier was required.

Above: This is one part of the end of Southend's pier in 1965. The two small boats could take sightseers for short river trips and behind them is the lifeboat's slipway. The 1976 fire destroyed all of these buildings.

Below: The *Golden Eagle* approaching Southend Pier, 1924. This was one of the ships that journeyed between Southend and the Kent towns of Ramsgate and Margate. The fashions of the onlookers are very much of that period and extremely formal. For many years, Ramsgate and Margate competed with Southend-on-Sea as holiday destinations for the citizens of London and its suburbs. *(Photograph by the author's father)*

Above: The newly rebuilt end of Southend Pier, taken from the PS *Waverley* as it started its journey to central London in 2003.

Below: Royal Terrace, 2003. This fine terrace with its lovely wrought-iron balconies, which was built between 1791 and 1793, stands beside the Royal Hotel and has fine views over the Thames. In 1805, Lady Emma Hamilton stayed in the Royal Terrace and held a ball there for Admiral Nelson.

Above: The Royal Hotel, 2003. Built in the 1790s, this is one of the oldest buildings in Southend. At first it was called the Grand Hotel, but after Caroline, Princess of Wales stayed there in 1804, the name was changed to the Royal Hotel. The building still exists but, as can be seen from this photograph, it no longer operates as a hotel but as a public house.

'Adventure Playground', 2003. This group of attractions and fairground
lies right beside the pier; in the past it has been known as 'Peter Pan's
playground'.

In the foreground is one of the modern fishing boats from Leigh-on-Sea, while the tall domed building dominating the horizon is the Kursaal. This photograph was taken from Southend Pier in 2003, and there is a row of white seabirds standing at the border between the mud and the river. The Kursaal was opened in 1901 and housed many different rides and amusements, although there had been fairground attractions in Southend by the latter part of the nineteenth century. The pier and the Kursaal are two buildings that are specifically associated with Southend-on-Sea. Southend's carnival float, known as the Kursaal Express, is described in chapter 2.

Above left: Seafront arcade, Southend, 1965. This arcade still exists more than thirty-five years later. All the photographs on this page and the page opposite were taken on the stretch of seafront (more precisely riverfront) between the pier and the Kursaal.

Below left: Seafront arcade, 2003.

Above right: Seafront arcade, 2003.

Below right: Seafront, *c.*1970. This photograph was taken on Boxing Day, which was one of the few occasions when the amusement machines and other attractions were closed. However, things have changed and such closures are unlikely to occur in this day and age; the front is normally thronging with people. Compared to the scenes above, the buildings look very dated. The pub boasts Charrington's name, but that brewer has long since ceased to brew beer.

Above left: Between the pier and the Kursaal there is a stretch of road comprising arcades, pubs and restaurants. This photograph, taken in 2001, comprises all three. On the left is Las Vegas, which is an outlet with arcade games; in the centre is a traditional pub, the Falcon; and on the right is the Las Vegas grill serving fish and chips.

Below left: Photographed about 1970, the signs show some of the popular food on sale at that time. Rock is a confectionery stick typical of many seaside resorts.

Above right: The Arcadian Bars were photographed about 1970 and they occupied a lovely old building with these wrought-iron balconies.

Below right: Originally, the main centre in this area was Prittlewell, and South End was simply a very small fishing community. It began to develop during the latter part of the eighteenth century and one the first buildings was the Hope Hotel. It was built around 1790 and has changed little externally. This photograph was taken in 2001.

Above: Southend Airport, *c.*1970. The letters on the main aircraft, BUA, stood for British United Airways. The aircraft was known as a Carvair and had been converted into that marque from a Douglas DC4 by Aviation Traders Engineering Ltd based at Southend Airport. The aircraft was designed to carry a few cars and made journeys between Southend and Ostende and Southend and Basle. It entered service in 1962 and continued until 1976. Presumably price competition from the ferry companies was an important factor in ending this service.

Below: A Vickers Viscount operated by British Midland Airways at Southend Airport, about 1980. Almost certainly this aircraft had just flown in from the Channel Islands, as BMA had immediately taken over this route once Channel Airways stopped operating. The Viscount was Britain's most popular post-war aircraft with some 440 being built in the period 1950 to 1964. It was the world's first turboprop airliner being powered by four Rolls Royce Dart engines and thereby broke the monopoly of piston-powered passenger aircraft. It brought new standards of comfort to passengers with a pressurised cabin, a cruising speed of 324mph and an operating ceiling approaching 30,000 feet. The size of the passenger compartment was gradually increased until it carried some sixty passengers.

At one time Southend was a busy regional airport and it reached a peak in 1967 when it handled nearly 700,000 passengers per year. Nowadays the numbers are minimal. In order to boost business it has renamed itself as London Southend and there are currently (2003) plans to develop the airport to make it once again an important flight centre.

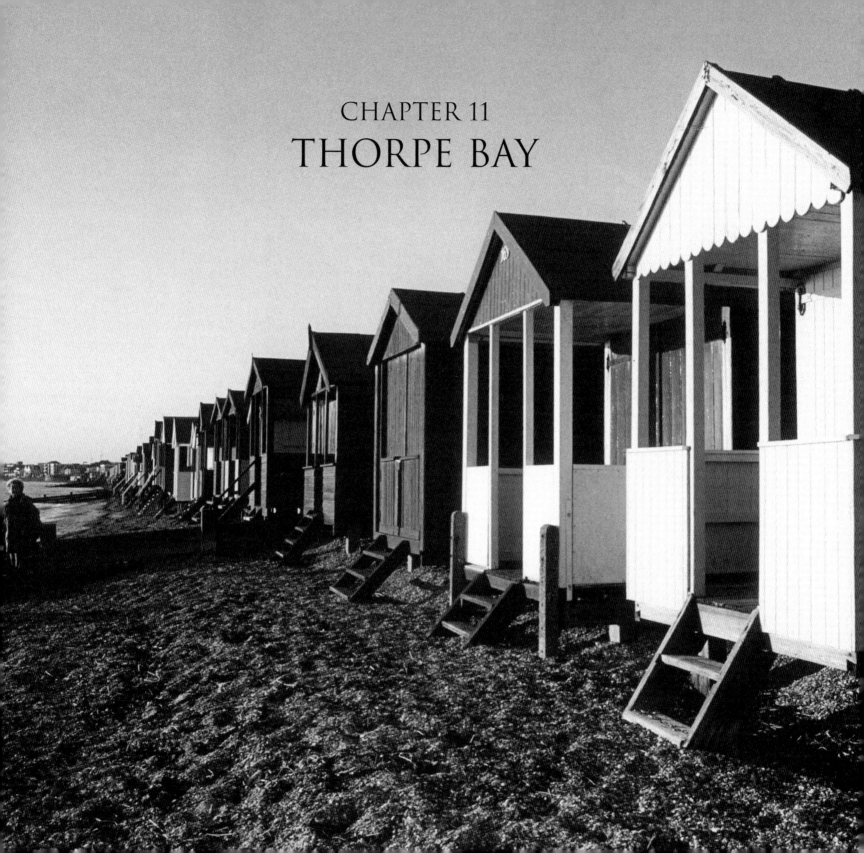

CHAPTER 11
THORPE BAY

Previous page: Beach huts, Thorpe Bay, 2003. Beach huts are a major feature of the riverfront in Thorpe Bay and appear in subsequent photographs.

Thorpe Bay is some two miles east of Southend-on-Sea, and is the nearest point to the mouth of the river reached in this book. There were plans for an upmarket residential area called (eventually) Thorpe Bay before the First World War, but its implementation was delayed until after the conflict. Even the name, Thorpe Bay, was chosen to convey the feeling of a district having better housing and other

amenities. It has a simple river frontage with no shops or kiosks and some greensward.

Above: Yachtsmen, Thorpe Bay, *c.*1970. Thorpe Bay is a major centre for yachting, which plays an important role in the use of the river. At this point the river is used almost solely for recreational purposes, as witnessed by these photographs of sailing and by the very large number of beach huts.

Thorpe Bay, 1969. These two yachts are returning towards the slipway used by Thorpe Bay Yacht Club as the day's sailing comes to an end. Shortly after this the two sailing boats will be pulled from the water.

Above: Thorpe Bay, 1969. This photograph was taken on a Sunday evening when the day's sailing was coming to a close. The two photographs on this page show some of the sailors undertaking the task of pulling their yachts up the ramp or slipway.

Below: Thorpe Bay, 1969.

Opposite: Thorpe Bay, 1963. This photograph shows the proximity between Thorpe Bay and Southend. It is looking upriver and on the horizon is Southend Pier. This view was taken when the tide was low, as the small boats are standing on the mud. In the foreground the dark shapes are some of the beach huts which line the front at Thorpe Bay.

Above: Thorpe Bay, 1963. This is another view towards Southend. The pier is just visible on the horizon and more beach huts can be seen below the roadway. Just noticeable in the middle of the horizon is a gasometer (a storage holder used for town gas). This has since been demolished. In 1963 there were no yellow lines, no bus lanes and indeed very few cars.

Below: Beach huts, Thorpe Bay, 2003. This view is looking to the mouth of the river and out to sea. This view has changed little over the past four decades save for the addition of extra groynes and the radio aerial in the distance. It is possible that the mast is used for portable telephones.

Beach huts, Thorpe Bay, 2003. These huts are one of the really noticeable features of the beach at Thorpe Bay. They provide shelter from poor weather, some privacy and users are able to brew a cup of tea whenever they wish. However, they have few other modern conveniences. Nevertheless, ownership and usage of these huts is prized and when one becomes available they often sell for quite considerable sums of money.

Above: Taken one evening *c.*1970, this photograph shows another advantage of the low tide, as it is possible for horse riders to venture upon the mud.

Below: The horse riders continued riding further away from the land until eventually it was possible to photograph them along with the end of Southend Pier. This upriver view is looking west which means that there are, sometimes, stunning sunset scenes. The effect of the light on this particular evening was such that no distant objects could be seen and even the Kent coast was hidden from view.

Left: This is an evening beach scene at Thorpe Bay, *c.*1970. It was also one of those occasions when the tide was in.

Top: This is another scene taken about 1970; note the flared jeans.

Bottom: This view, taken in 2003, is looking across the river towards the Kent bank and sums up the Thames' economic value. The tall chimney is part of the Isle of Grain Power Station and to the right is an industrial plant, both emphasising the usefulness of water transport for carrying bulk raw materials. The ship is a cargo vessel operated by Cobelfret Ferries, whose terminal is close to the Queen Elizabeth II Bridge.

The final photograph in this book is another view taken from Thorpe Bay, *c.*1970. It shows the sun setting over the end of the pier, several years before it was destroyed by fire.

This and the previous photographs provide a contrast in river usage. Many scenes show the continuing economic importance of the Thames while the view on the left sums up the romantic side of the river and its recreational use.